D1606602

Who Will Come to the Leprechaun's Lunch?

Written and illustrated by
Annie Lena Day

-To my grandson, Owen, who loves to be creative.

Copyright 2024 by Annie Lena Day
All rights reserved.

No part of this book may be reproduced in any form or by any electronic or mechanical means, including informational storage and retrieval systems, without written permission from the author, except for the use of brief quotations in a book review.

ISBN: 9798850757939

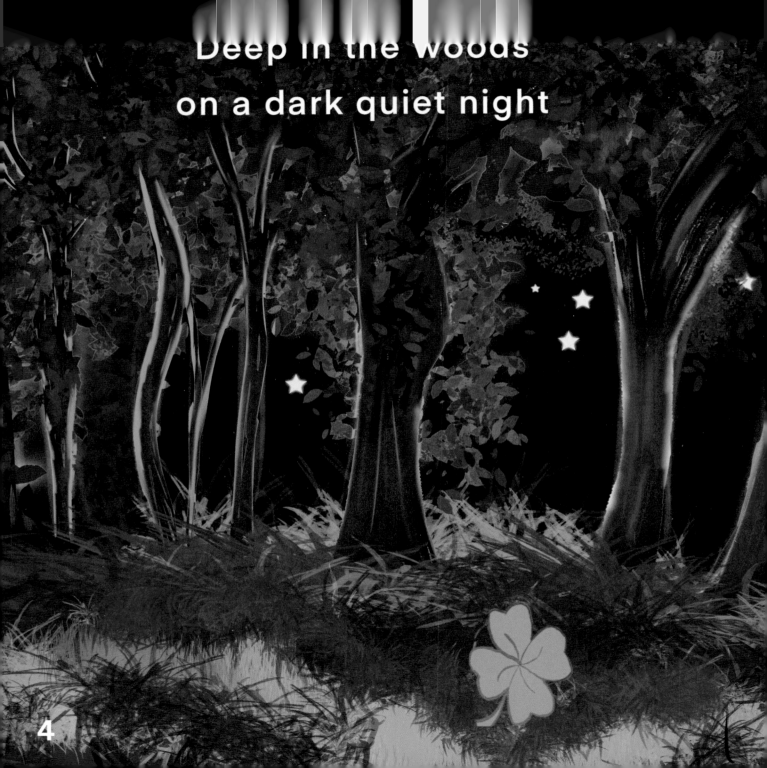

Deep in the woods
on a dark quiet night

a leprechaun danced
by the moon's bright light.

As he danced a fine jig
he heard not a sound.

Not a clap.
Not a cheer.

For no one was near.

His friends were all hiding
and rightly so.
He tricked them all once.
Maybe more.
I don't know.

There's a magic in dance.
And a magic in song.
But with no one to share it,
it just seemed very wrong.

He looked at his gold
so shiny and bright.

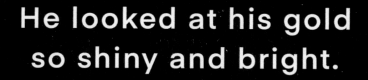

But he knew that something
just wasn't quite right.

9

He thought of his friends,

once near

now far.

He remembered the laughter
and the fun that they had.

But he remembered many things
he had done that were bad.

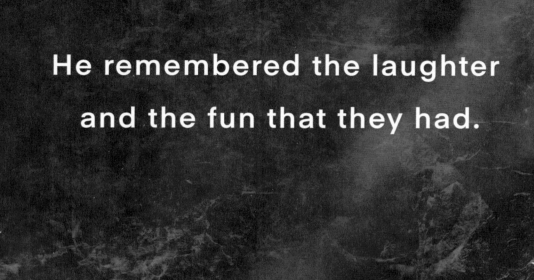

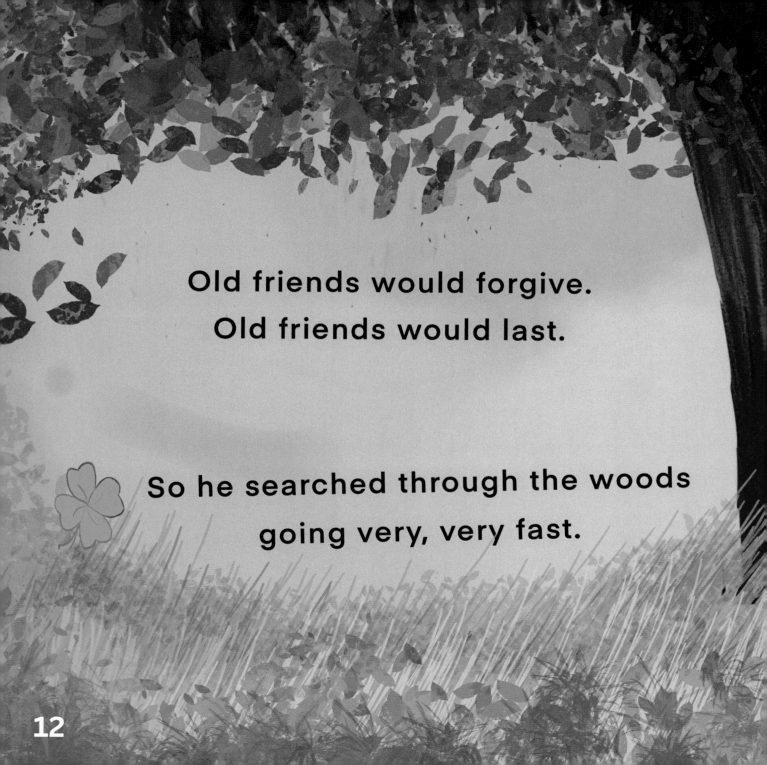

Old friends would forgive.
Old friends would last.

So he searched through the woods
going very, very fast.

He searched high in the sky
and down low

in a

hole

At last he found
the Grumpy Old Troll. 13

"My friend, my friend,
Come with me!
Come with me!

We'll dance, sing, and play
all the night and the day."

14

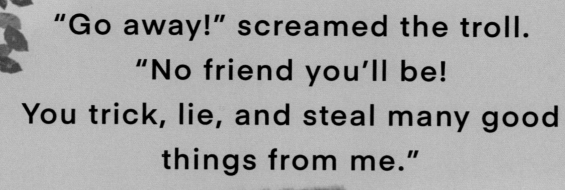

"Go away!" screamed the troll.
"No friend you'll be!
You trick, lie, and steal many good
things from me."

"I've changed. I've changed.
There won't be any tricks.
A lunch will be served at
quarter to six."

"A lunch so late is not a date.
Perhaps I'll come.
Perhaps I'll be late."

With a wink and a smile,

18

he vanished so quick.

"I'll see you real soon.
There won't be a trick."

In the field full of shamrocks
where the fairies all live,
flew a fairy so gentle
many smiles did she give.

With a click of his heels
and a spin on his toes,

20

he went straight to the land
and reached out for her hand.

He sang very sweet.
He sang very low.

The fairy, she danced
and spun on her toe.

When the music had stopped
and the air was all still,
she looked deep in his eye.
Then said, "Oh!
Oh my!

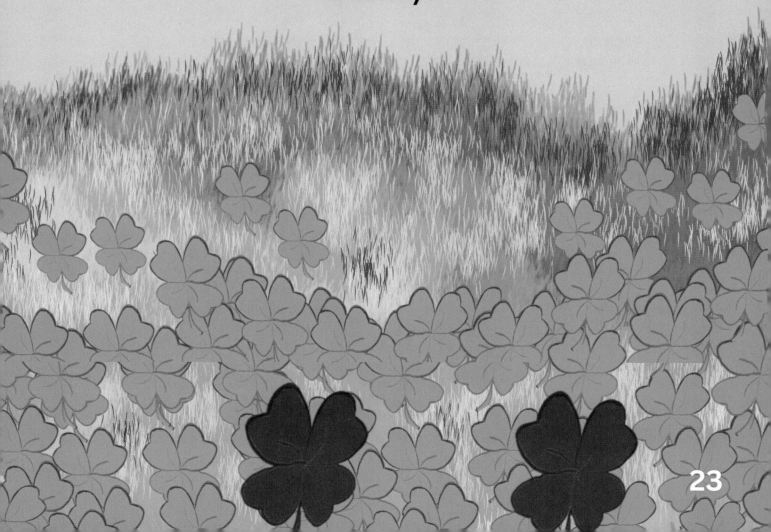

I remember you now.
I remember you well.
I remember the stories
and lies that you tell."

"I've changed. I've changed.
There won't be any tricks.
Lunch will be served
at quarter to six."

"A lunch so late is not a date.
Perhaps I'll come.
Perhaps I'll be late."

He smiled and laughed
and vanished so quick.

"I'll see you real soon.
There won't be a trick."

27

Now off to the cave
to find the old hag.

'Tis true she is mean
and ugly to see
But still a good friend to me
she could be.

"Go away!" screamed the hag.
"No friend you'll be.
You trick, lie, and steal many
good things from me."

"Tis true I've played many a trick
but this time I'll make
our friendship stick.

A lunch will be served
at quarter to six."

A lunch so late is not a date.
Perhaps I'll come.
Perhaps I'll be late.

With magic and a snap

to his home he went back.

32

First he built a great fire
and he melted his gold.

Then arose lots of magic
like times of the old.

It reached up to the clouds.
Then it spun like a top.

The top turned to
a ....

table!

And it floated

a while,

as the leprechaun found
some shoes with great style.

37

The table
descended
right down
to the

ground
and landed on top
of the shoes that were found.

Then he sat and he thought
and he knew what he'd need.

He must gather some food
with the utmost speed.

He chopped potatoes for fries,

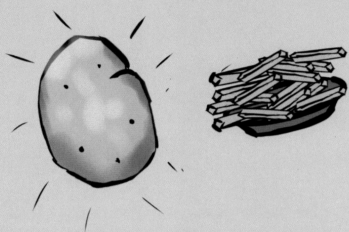

brewed dandelion tea,

baked cupcakes real tall

creating food for all.

Now music he needed
and music he'd get.

So he built a fine flute

and the wind sang a song.
He hoped that the guests
would soon come along.

At precisely six
and NOT quarter 'til,
the creatures all walked
to the top of the hill.

The leprechaun smiled
and welcomed them all,

as he showed them the table
with food piled tall.

As they danced and they sang
thru the day and the night,

46

sweet notes filled the sky
and the land with delight.

When all were tired
and tummies were full,

a rainbow appeared
right out of the blue.

Then the magic that only the forgiven know

50

made a rainbow of hearts
fall on friends down below.

Talking and Thinking

1. Legend says leprechauns like to make shoes and this leprechaun is looking for ones with "great style".

Style is a matter of opinion. Look back in the book on page 37. Which shoes do you think have great style?

2. Which characters would you like to be friends with (the leprechaun, the old hag, the grumpy old troll, the fairy)?

3. Do you think the leprechaun will do tricks in the future?

Will he tell lies?

Will he steal?

4. A shamrock is on each page. Some are hiding, but some are easy to find.

Look back through the book to find them.

Parents,
If your child enjoyed this book, please leave a review so others can enjoy it too. Thanks!

May your day be touched by
some Irish luck.

Annie Lena Day is an author and illustrator who also likes to teach and narrate stories.

Made in the USA
Middletown, DE
11 March 2024

51273436R00031